FAITH TAKES BACK WHAT THE DEVIL'S STOLEN

By Kenneth Hagin Jr.

Chapter 1
RESPONDING TO GOD'S GIFTS

The other day I began thinking about the word "take," and I began to realize that things have to be *taken* in the spiritual realm. They don't just fall on you. You have to reach out and take them.

Salvation is an example. Did any of you get saved without reaching out and taking what God was offering you? Did salvation just fall on you? Or did you respond and reach out and take the gift God was offering you in salvation?

How many businessmen attain success without going out and taking it? Do they just sit back in their offices, put their feet up on their desks, and say, "Well, I'm a businessman. I know all the business principles" — and have big business deals fall on them? Not often. They are successful because they go out, take hold of situations, and make them work.

It seems that man is programmed to be a success. Do any of you *not* want to succeed? I've never met anybody who didn't want to succeed, have you? Everybody I've ever met has wanted to be a success.

Some people may say they don't want to be a success, but don't listen to their words. Watch their actions. Their actions prove they want to be a success, because they're out there striving for it every day.

Success comes when an individual

realizes what he has, who he is, and what abilities he possesses in the natural. Then he takes those abilities and surrounds himself with people who have abilities in areas where he is weak. They make a strong team and go out and take success.

Usually, if you study business partners closely, you will find that one has expertise in one area and his partner has expertise in another area. Put them together, and they have expertise in all areas of their business. If they need more expertise, they'll go out and find department heads or supervisors to handle those jobs. And they become successful.

I'm talking about natural things here. I like to bring things down to where you can see the parallel between success in the natural and success in the spiritual life.

Most people try to divorce the two, putting natural life in one corner and spiritual life in another. But the truth is: You are a *natural* human being. You live in a natural world. At the same time, however, you are a *spiritual* being — a spirit. You live in a spirit world. You must learn to combine the two with God and become an explosive force in both areas of your life.

That's where the word "take" comes in. It's a small word, "take."

When I say the word "take," most people immediately get a visual impression in their minds. Whether you realize it or not, when you hear a word, it automatically triggers a memory bank in this computer brain of ours, and that memory bank brings up a certain definition or image of that word. Different people see different pictures.

When I hear the word "take," the image it triggers in my mind is a hand reaching out taking hold of something. What kind of mental picture do you get?

It doesn't matter which translation of the Bible you own; it still contains 32,000 promises made by God Himself. For whom did Jesus purchase these 32,000 promises? For God? For the angels? No, they don't need them. Jesus purchased them for the Church of the Lord Jesus Christ — the *ecclesia* — the called-out ones.

God gave us Jesus: all that He is, all that He has, and all that He has done. That's what has been given to the Church. Second Peter 1:3 says, *"According as his divine power hath given unto us all things that pertain unto life and godliness . . . ."* Notice the word "hath" in that Scripture. Is "hath" past tense, present tense, or future tense? *Past!*

If someone "hath" (or has) done something for you, it's yours. If God "hath" given unto us all things that pertain to life and godliness, how should we respond?

Suppose I'm away from home holding a service, and a delivery boy walks through the door of the church and says, "Telegram for you." I open that telegram and it announces that the richest man in the world has read one of my books — he likes me — and he has put $1 million into my bank account in Tulsa, Oklahoma. Everybody would praise God with me, wouldn't they?

But suppose the next day you accompany me to the airport and I sit in the waiting room whining and complaining, "I sure would like to go back to Tulsa! I sure would like to go back home, but I haven't got a ticket."

You'd say, "Hey, I thought you had $1 million down there in your bank account! You got that telegram while you were here. The money's yours."

"Oh, yes. I know that. I sure wish I could get home."

You'd think something was the matter with me if I said that. You would know all I had to do was go to the counter and purchase a ticket, write out a check, or charge it — because I had money in the bank to back it.

Well, what is the difference between that and spiritual things? God *hath* already given us everything that pertaineth to life and godliness. What are we sitting around for, whining, crying, and saying to one another, "I just don't know what is going to happen. I don't know if I'm going to be able to make it or not. The devil has been after me. My life is so torn up!"

That's what a lot of people are doing! I didn't say they aren't born again. I didn't say they aren't filled with the Spirit. They *have* already been given everything that pertains to life and godliness.

That's where the word "take" comes in. By faith reach out and *take* what belongs to you. Begin to live in the success, happiness, and liberty of the power of the Word of God. *Faith takes it!*

Someone wrote that the word "receive" in Mark 11:24 could be translated "take with force" or "seize with a grip that cannot be shaken loose."

Receive what God has for you. How? By reaching up in faith and taking it! The problem is that most people are waiting for God to hover over them like you do over your flowers. They're waiting for God to stand over the top of them with a little watering pot. Then they'll get excited and say, "God just poured me out a blessing!"

No, God poured out a blessing on the Church some 2,000 years ago when Jesus Christ Himself, suspended between heaven and earth on that rugged cross, said, "It is finished."

Jesus died, went into the pits of hell, and fought with the enemy. Then He rose victorious over death, hell, and the grave, ascended, and sat down at the right hand of the Father. He purchased all there is in life and godliness — and He has given it to the Church.

We don't have to wait for God to come by and pour us out a blessing! All we have to do is know who we are in Christ, what we are in Christ, what the Word of God says, reach up, and take what belongs to us!

The Holy Spirit could say to us, like the angels said to those who were gazing heavenward after Jesus' ascension, *"Why stand ye gazing up into heaven? this same Jesus, which is taken up from you into heaven, shall so come in like manner as ye have seen him go into heaven"* (Acts 1:11). Then the angels added, "Now go do what He told you to do."

Too often Christians are sitting here in this world, gazing off into the far blue yonder, looking for some kind of "pie in the sky," singing about "the sweet by-and-by," or talking about how great it's going to be "on the other side."

It's going to be good — and I thank God for it — but what I'm interested in is what can help me in the now. *Now* is when I'm living. *Now* is when I need something to carry me through the energy crisis, economic recession, etc. — not in the sweet by-and-by. Thank God for the promise of heaven — I need that as inspiration to keep me going — but I need something to carry me right now in the face of the darkness of this world.

The Word of God says *"take it!"*

Chapter 2
THINGS THAT SHAKE FAITH

If we go to the story of Peter walking on the water, we find that once he stepped outside the boat, he really did begin to walk on the water. But what happened when he took his attention off of Jesus and the power and faith of God? What happened when Peter began to look at a bank of waves on one side of him — and then saw another bank of waves on the other side?

As long as Peter kept his eyes on Jesus, he walked up and over the crest of those waves — but when the next wave looked like it was going to break over him, Peter began to sink.

The same circumstances that caused Peter to sink are robbing modern Christians of their happiness and joy and are keeping us from taking what God already has given us by faith. Like Peter, we have begun to look, listen, and feel the power of the enemy. We have gotten our eyes off of God and the things of God. The waves of depression, sadness, sickness, disease, and short bank accounts have become a part of our life.

The first thing that is robbing us is the things we *feel*. Peter *felt* the wind blowing on him. You can't see the wind, but you can feel the effects of it. In that way, it's like the Holy Spirit. You can't see the Holy Spirit, but you certainly can see the effects of the Holy Spirit, for He is tangible, just like the wind is.

Second, Peter was affected by the things he *saw*. He saw the threatening waves. What kinds of things do we see in the '80s to shake our faith? We see television newscasts and newspapers and magazines filled with reports of fear, doubt, unbelief, and depression. We feel the pinch of inflation every time we go to the grocery store or pull into a gas station.

But I want you to know that you can reach up by the hand of faith and take what belongs to you. You can begin to claim God's promises. You do not have to be swept under by depression or the crises of this world.

I don't know how God is going to do it, but in His Word He has promised He shall supply *all your need according to his riches in glory by Christ Jesus* (Phil. 4:19).

In the summer of 1980, the crusade team and I traveled from Oklahoma to California, up the West Coast of Canada, and then all the way across Canada. Somebody asked me, "Aren't you afraid? They've been talking about a fuel shortage. What if you get your bus out there in the middle of the desert and you can't buy gas?"

I replied, "God took care of the children of Israel. As long as they believed Him, they walked across the burning sand, and not one ounce of shoe leather was burned off of the bottom of those sandals they were wearing. My God is the same God today. He's still the same Jehovah who carried the children of Israel. He is still *El Shaddai* — the God who is more than enough.

"And if He has to, He will *manufacture* diesel in that fuel tank — and we'll carry the Gospel of the Lord Jesus Christ. I am scheduling *more* crusades, as a matter of fact. I've alerted the crusade team to be ready for them."

I'm going to take what is rightfully mine. The Word of God says it's mine. I've read this Book. This Book tells me that it belongs to me, and I'm not about to let the devil steal what belongs to me.

Suppose you drove up to your house and found a moving van backed up to your door and men busy moving all your belongings out of the house. You would ask, "What is going on here?"

Suppose a man walked up to you and said, "Here's the deed. This says the house belongs to me, and I'm moving in. I've sold all this furniture, and I'm moving it out. I'm going to be moving my furniture in and living here."

You wouldn't walk back to your car and say to your wife, "Well, honey, I thought that this was our house, but that man has a piece of paper that says it belongs to him. I don't know how it happened. We paid it off last year, but I guess it belongs to him, so we might as well go down to Aunt Mary's and see if they'll let us spend the night until I can figure out something to do."

Not one of you would do this. You would go to the proper authorities and find out what was going on. Yet what are we, as the Church of the Lord Jesus Christ, doing when the devil comes by, backs up his moving van, and steals our joy while moving in his sickness and disease?

We say, "Well, I *thought* the Lord was going to take care of me, but I guess He isn't." That's what is the matter with us; we are allowing the devil to rob us needlessly. God already *has* given us *all* things that pertain to godliness and happiness and life.

This verse says that all of us can live in happiness. It says that all of us can live in prosperity. It says that all of us can live in health. It says that all of us can live with spiritual authority. It says that all of us have become joint-heirs with Jesus Christ. We are the sons of God!

When the devil backs his moving van up to my property, I look him square in the eye and say, "Hey — didn't you see that NO TRESPASSING sign out there? Get your moving van out of here. Pack your goods up, Mr. Devil. You have no right and no authority to come in and steal my happiness, my health, my joy, my finances, and my prosperity. I have taken them by faith. God said they are mine. You have no right and no authority to them."

That's what you would tell that man if he backed a moving van up to your house unbidden. You would say, "This is mine. You have no authority — you have no right — here." And you would run him off the place.

Do the same thing with the Word of God when the devil comes to steal what belongs to you! Take the Word of God and begin to say, "It is written, Mr. Devil. It is written . . . I take it by the Word of God and by faith." (You will find that the Word of God says in Matthew 11:12 that the violent take the kingdom by force.)

It reminds me of a story I heard Dad tell. He said it came from Smith Wigglesworth.

A woman left her house one day and

started walking down the street to wait for a bus. Her little old dog followed her. The woman looked at the dog and said, "Now, honey, you can't go today. Go back to the house."

The little old dog didn't pay any attention. It just wagged its tail more and kept trotting right behind her.

The woman stopped again, looked back, and said, "Now, honey, you can't go today. Go on back to the house."

She proceeded on down the street and waited on the corner for the bus. That little old dog just walked around her, his tail flopping, licking her on the feet and sitting there, panting, looking up at her, like little old dogs do.

By this time, the bus was coming down the street. The woman looked at the dog and said, "GET BACK UP TO THE HOUSE!" And that dog tucked its tail between its legs and — zoom! — it got back on that front porch in a hurry.

Smith Wigglesworth said, "That's the way you have to deal with the devil. He'll take all that 'honey' business you want to give him. But if you really mean business, take the Word of God and say, 'It is written. Get out of here, devil! I resist you in the Name of Jesus!' And you will get results."

Chapter 3
HANDLING CONTRADICTORY THOUGHTS

We must quickly cast away every thought that is contrary to the Word of God. No, you can't keep a bird from flying over your head, but you certainly can keep it from building a nest in your hair!

When you start this walk of faith and start to take things by faith, you can't keep the devil from bringing his contradictory thoughts and contradictory circumstances for you to see — but you can refuse to think on them.

You can combat his devices by quoting, "It is written. It is written. I take what belongs to me, Mr. Devil, because the Word says that no weapon formed against me will prosper (Isa. 54:17). The Word says, Mr. Devil, that my body is healed by the power of God. It is written, Mr. Devil, that my every need is met."

We've got nearly 2,000 students in RHEMA Bible Training Center in Tulsa, Oklahoma. Our 74-acre campus has $7½ million worth of improvements and buildings on it. They didn't get there by my sitting around my office saying, "Well, I guess if the Lord wants us to have it, He will give it to us."

No, those improvements got there by Dr. Hagin, myself, and a lot of other people taking the Word of God and delivering it in the devil's face whenever the outflow was more than the income.

Once I was caught in a terrible cash flow crunch. If I had listened to the enemy, who had begun to camp on my shoulder and talk in my ear, I still would be hiding under my desk, afraid to stick my head out. I would listen to that old boy about all

I could, and then I would jump to my feet and say, "Mr. Devil, GET OUT OF HERE! GET OUT OF MY OFFICE!"

I have actually kicked him out just like that. "GET OUT OF MY OFFICE! IT IS WRITTEN! IT IS WRITTEN! IT IS WRITTEN! I TAKE WHAT GOD HAS PROMISED ME! I TAKE IT BY FAITH!"

And he would reply, "But where is the money coming from?"

I would answer, "I don't know where it's coming from. That's not my part of the contract. My part of the contract is to believe God. It's God's part to make it come true. And the Word of God says that He never fails. He never has failed up until now, and He's not going to fail me now, Mr. Devil. So get out of here!"

He'll take off for a while, but he won't stay gone long. He soon comes back, battering at the same door. If you don't keep reinforcing that door with the faith it takes, he eventually will batter it down.

And if he ever batters it down and gets his foot in the door, you are in trouble. *The best way to combat the devil is not to let him get a foothold in the first place!*

For example, how many of you have ever wakened with a little scratching sensation in your throat? Usually we tend to ignore it, hoping it will go away. But by the end of the day, if we haven't dealt with it, the thing will have hold of you. It is harder to get your healing then, after it has hold of you, than it is in the morning when you have that first symptom.

Grab the Word of God and run the enemy away before he ever gets a good start unpacking. (It's always easier to move somebody out of a room *before* they unpack.)

Take it by faith. Symptoms may linger — you may have to clear your throat — but don't pay any attention to the symptoms.

Remember, the fig tree in the Bible story was dead when Jesus cursed it, even though its leaves still were waving green in the breeze. It wasn't until 24 hours later that those leaves turned brown and the disciples noticed it had died. The tree actually died when Jesus cursed it.

The minute you first reach out by faith and take hold of that sickness, disease, or whatever, and command it to turn loose, it becomes a reality in the spirit world. Your constant holding fast to your confession will bring it into reality in the natural, physical world in which you live.

The thing that stops most people when they reach out and take hold of what they need by faith is that their grasp is weak. Remember, God already has given you 32,000 promises. He *hath* already given you all that pertains to life and godliness. What you must do by faith to receive these promises is reach out and grab them with a grip that can't be shaken by the least wind, wave, or any other contradictory circumstance. Hold onto these promises.

Yes, you may feel like your situation is holding you rather than you are holding it, but keep confessing God's Word. Say, "I've taken it by faith. It belongs to me. The Word says so."

Soon you will have hold of what you are believing God for. The contradictory circumstances will be gone, and you'll be walking on to another victory. Then you'll reach out by faith and grab hold of something else, and you'll conquer it. Soon you'll reach out and grab something else and conquer it, too. And you'll keep walking, confessing, climbing, climbing, climbing.

No, there never is a plateau. You will continue to climb until the day Jesus Christ splits the clouds of glory and takes us out of this world. There should be a continual taking by faith and living with the power of God in your life.

This happiness — this abundant life — belongs to you. Take it by faith. It is yours today. It is up to you — not God — whether or not it becomes a reality in your life.

God has said in His Word that He HATH given us all things that pertain to life and godliness. ALL things. (He healeth ALL our diseases, not part of them.)

Did He say in His Word that He would meet our immediate needs, but we would have to meet our little needs ourselves? Or did He say He would meet ALL of our needs? He said He would meet ALL of our needs.

Chapter 4
FAITH TAKES

God is reaching His hand down from heaven, saying, "My child, here's all you ever needed to have happiness, godliness, and a joyous life on earth. Here it is! Here it is!"

You can look at that hand and say "Oh, I wish that were so. Oh, wouldn't that be nice!" Or you can, by faith, reach up and grab hold of all the provisions of life God's hand is offering you.

With your other hand, grab hold of the things that hinder you from enjoying godliness, health, wealth, and happiness. Your faith will activate God's power, and that power will flow through you to set you free from those hindrances.

BUT NEVER RELEASE YOUR HOLD ON GOD AS HE REACHES DOWN AND OFFERS THE PROVISIONS OF LIFE TO YOU.

You see, God's not going to come hit you over the head with a 20-pound sledgehammer and say, "Son, get in line. Here it is. Take it." He's not going to drop it on you. He's not going to spoon-feed you and force it down your mouth. No, all He's going to do is offer it. It's there.

YOU MUST TAKE IT BY FAITH. FAITH TAKES.

And after faith takes, FAITH NEVER TURNS LOOSE. And because faith never turns loose, it leads to success by the power of God.

Begin to talk to God. Whatever it is you need, quote the Scriptures to Him.

If it's finances, quote Scriptures about finances to Him. If it's healing you need, quote Scriptures about healing to Him. Remind Him that He "hath" given to us all that pertains to life and godliness.

Tell Him you are taking what belongs to you by faith, and you will never again relinquish what belongs to you in the Name of Jesus.

Because He HATH purchased for us ALL that pertains to life and godliness, we can now reach up by the power of the Word of God and take what belongs to us and walk in victory in Christ Jesus.

Faith rejoices now — not when you see it happen or manifest.

In one of my dad's meetings years ago, a little old man went down to the altar one Sunday and "claimed" his wife's salvation. After he claimed it by faith, he had a great Pentecostal time — a hilarious time — like the joyous time they had on the Day of Pentecost. You see, *by faith he took it then.*

A few days later, his wife attended church with him, went to the altar, and prayed through to salvation.

That night, her husband sat in the

back of the church with his arms folded, just looking at her. The other church members, because they had been praying for her for a long time, were ecstatic. (She was the meanest woman in town, according to the story.)

Somebody finally asked her husband, "Aren't you excited? That's your wife down there."

He replied, "Remember the other night when I got excited? I accepted it by faith then. I saw it then. It's 'old news' now. Why should I get excited now? It *happened* a week ago."

That's what faith does. *Faith rejoices at the moment of taking*. Faith doesn't rejoice when it manifests, because it's "old news" then — it already has taken place.

Do what you would do if you saw it happen this very moment — if you saw it take place in front of your eyes at this moment.

As you walk this great walk of faith,

never again say, "I don't know if I'm going to make it or not."

From now on, talk in faith and take it by faith. It may look bleak, but never relinquish your hold. Once you start out in faith, hold fast to your confession and praise God all the way to victory. Keep taking. Keep conquering the enemy. Keep winning more people to Jesus.

Take it by faith. Run with it like a dog runs off with a bone!

Rejoice because you have everything that pertains to life and godliness. It is yours. Live like it — rejoice in it — and have a good time on the way to heaven.

A Sinner's Prayer
To Receive Jesus As Savior

Dear Heavenly Father . . .

I come to you in the name of Jesus.

Your Word says, " . . . *him that cometh to me I will in no wise cast out*" (John 6:37),

So I know you won't cast me out,
    but you take me in,

And I thank you for it.

You said in your Word, "*Whosoever shall call upon the name of the Lord shall be saved*" (Rom. 10:13).

I am calling on your name,

So I know you have saved me now.

You also said, "*if thou shalt confess with thy mouth the Lord Jesus, and shalt believe in thine heart that God hath raised him from the dead, thou shalt be saved. For with the heart man believeth unto righteousness; and with the mouth confession is made unto salvation*" (Romans 10:9-10).

I believe in my heart Jesus Christ is the Son of God.

I believe that He was raised from the dead for my justification.

And I confess Him now as my Lord,

Because your Word says, " . . . *with the heart man believeth unto righteousness* . . . " and I do believe with my heart,

I have now become the righteousness of God in Christ (2 Cor. 5:21) . . . And I am saved!

Thank you, Lord!

Signed _____

Date _____